Cotton Mather

Author, Clergyman, and Scholar

Colonial Leaders

Lord Baltimore *English Politician and Colonist*

Benjamin Banneker *American Mathematician and Astronomer*

William Bradford *Governor of Plymouth Colony*

Benjamin Franklin *American Statesman, Scientist, and Writer*

Anne Hutchinson *Religious Leader*

Cotton Mather *Author, Clergyman, and Scholar*

William Penn *Founder of Democracy*

John Smith *English Explorer and Colonist*

Miles Standish *Plymouth Colony Leader*

Peter Stuyvesant *Dutch Military Leader*

Revolutionary War Leaders

Benedict Arnold *Traitor to the Cause*

Nathan Hale *Revolutionary Hero*

Alexander Hamilton *First U.S. Secretary of the Treasury*

Patrick Henry *American Statesman and Speaker*

Thomas Jefferson *Author of the Declaration of Independence*

John Paul Jones *Father of the U.S. Navy*

Thomas Paine *Political Writer*

Paul Revere *American Patriot*

Betsy Ross *American Patriot*

George Washington *First U.S. President*

Cotton Mather

Author, Clergyman, and Scholar

Norma Jean Lutz

Arthur M. Schlesinger, jr.
Senior Consulting Editor

Chelsea House Publishers

Philadelphia

Produced by Robert Gerson Publisher's Services, Avondale, PA

CHELSEA HOUSE PUBLISHERS
Editor in Chief Stephen Reginald
Production Manager Pamela Loos
Director of Photography Judy L. Hasday
Art Director Sara Davis
Managing Editor James D. Gallagher

Staff for *COTTON MATHER*
Project Editor Anne Hill
Project Editor/Publishing Coordinator Jim McAvoy
Contributing Editor Amy Handy
Associate Art Director Takeshi Takahashi
Series Design Keith Trego

The Chelsea House World Wide Web address is http://www.chelseahouse.com

First Printing
1 3 5 7 9 8 6 4 2

Library of Congress Cataloging-in-Publication Data

Lutz, Norma Jean.
Cotton Mather / by Norma Jean Lutz.
    p. cm. — (Colonial leaders)
Includes bibliographical references and index.
ISBN 0-7910-5343-1 (hc); 0-7910-5686-4 (pb)
1. Mather, Cotton, 1663-1728 Juvenile literature. 2. Puritans—Massachusetts
Biography Juvenile literature. 3. Massachusetts—History—Colonial period,
ca. 1600-1775 Juvenile literature.
I. Title. II. Series.
F67.M43L88 1999
285.8'092—dc21
[B]   99-25344
                                                                CIP

To Donovan Eastburn, with love from your great aunt

> **Publisher's Note:** In Colonial and Revolutionary War America,
> there were no standard rules for spelling, punctuation, capitaliza-
> tion, or grammar. Some of the quotations that appear in the Colo-
> nial Leaders and Revolutionary War Leaders series come from
> original documents and letters written during this time in history.
> Original quotations reflect writing inconsistencies of the period.

Contents

Cotton Mather's father, Increase Mather, was a powerful preacher and an accomplished scholar. A deeply religious and highly intelligent man, he received the first doctor of divinity degree granted in America.

1

A Noble Heritage

When Cotton Mather was born in Boston on February 12, 1663, he was bound with a strange name. But he also had a notable heritage as big as all New England. Cotton Mather was the grandson of two of the most famous and powerful preachers in New England. Every day of his life, he felt the weight of that heritage and his responsibility to live up to it.

To the **Puritans** who lived in Boston in the early 1600s, two names were highly esteemed—John Cotton and Richard Mather. Both of these men had been active pastors in the Church of England; however, both men were **Nonconformists**, or Puritans.

Puritans believed that each person should seek God personally without the need for a priest. The Church of England frowned on such free thinking. Many Puritans were arrested and put into prison.

Because of these beliefs, John Cotton and Richard Mather were removed from their pastoral positions. In 1633 John Cotton sailed for New England and became pastor of First Church in Boston. He soon became the recognized head of the Congregational Church (a Puritan Church) in Boston.

Two years later, Richard Mather and his family were forced to leave England. Mather became pastor in the church in Dorchester just outside of Boston. In 1639 Richard and Katherine Mather gave birth to a son, whom they named Increase because of the great increase in freedom and good fortune they had experienced in the New World. Twenty-three years later, Increase Mather married Maria Cotton, daughter of John Cotton. Thus when their first child was born, he was given

Reverend John Cotton, Cotton Mather's grandfather, helped to establish the Puritan Church of
New England and headed the church in Boston.

the names of the two families: Cotton Mather.

From his earliest years, Cotton Mather was taught of the great accomplishments of his famous grandfathers, both of whom did much to form and establish the Puritan Church of New England. Richard Mather, along with two other pastors, translated the Psalms into English meter for singing. This was called the *Bay Psalm Book,* and was the first book printed in America.

In 1646 a convention of Puritan ministers met to draw up a platform for the Congregational Church government. The ministers included Ralph Partridge, John Cotton, and Richard Mather. This manual of rules was so well written, it was used for more than a hundred years. John Cotton and Richard Mather were also highly involved in the political matters of the day. They were prolific authors and, in later years, Cotton Mather's library shelves were filled with books authored by both his grandfathers.

After studying and preaching in England for a time, Cotton's father returned to Boston and became the preacher of a new church named Second Church, in the northern part of Boston. It was then that he married Maria Cotton. The newlyweds took up residence in the house of John Cotton, who had died in 1652. It was the house in which Maria had been born. Thus Cotton Mather grew up not only in the presence of his father, but in the lingering presence of his deceased grandfather as well.

The Boston of Cotton Mather's time was a small coastal village of about 7,000 people. The town was built upon a small peninsula attached to the mainland by the Boston Neck, a narrow band of land that was often covered by high tides or flood waters. When the neck was passable, ox-carts traveled the narrow road carrying firewood, charcoal, lumber, salted fish, furs, and produce into the town.

Long wharves stretched out into the harbor, and on them stood barrels and crates ready to be loaded onto the many ships that sailed in and out everyday. The narrow winding streets of Boston

Cotton Mather spent his childhood in Boston, which was small compared to today's standards. But even then it was an important harbor and business center.

were filled with shops and industries of all kinds—rope walks, carpenter shops, blacksmith shops, shoemaker shops, tanning pits, book stores, and printing shops. Cows still grazed on Boston Common and Indians strolled about the streets.

Cotton Mather grew up amid the sights, sounds, and smells of this bustling city. The Mather home was filled with books, prayers, study, and a great deal of family history. The home was also filled with love and gentleness. His father spent 16 hours a day in his study. Increase Mather felt that study and preaching were his vital missions in life. During church services, Cotton watched as his father preached

> **W**here there are sailing ships, there is a great need for strong ropes. Near the waterfront in colonial Boston, there were dozens of rope walks. Rope walks were sheds as much as three city blocks long. Here the workers walked up and down, twisting the hempen threads into ropes and cables many **fathoms** long.

with power and persuasion. Increase memorized every sermon and used no notes. In his father's study, Cotton listened as groups of Puritan ministers discussed and settled the governmental issues of the colony.

In time, nine children were born into this family: Cotton, Nathaniel, Maria, Elizabeth, Sarah, Samuel, Catherine, Hannah, and Abigail.

While many babies during colonial times died within the first year, only one Mather child, Catherine, died in childhood.

A quick learner and a natural student, Cotton was taught both at home and in what was known as a "dame school." This was an arrangement in which a woman of the community taught several children at a time in her home. Children were sent to dame school soon after age two. Cotton started his learning with a hornbook, a sheet of paper with the alphabet, a group of simple syllables, and the Lord's Prayer written on it, which was placed over a tablet of wood. A sheet of transparent cow's horn, which had a yellowish color, was placed over the paper. Hornbooks were tied to the child's side or around their neck, so they were never misplaced.

Later Cotton attended Boston Latin School, where his instructor was the famous Boston schoolmaster Ezekiel Cheever. While Cheever was known for frequently beating schoolboys, he noted that Cotton Mather was a student who

The A.B.C

set forthe by the Rynges maiestie and his Clergye, and commaunded to be taught through out all his Realme. All other vtterly set a part, as the teachers thereof tender his graces fauour.

A.a.b.c.d.e.f.g.h.i.k.l.m. n.o.p.q.r.s.s.t.u.v.w.x. y.z.&.∴: Est. Amen.

A.B.C.D.E.F.G.H.I.K.L. M.N.O.P.Q.R.S.T.U.W. X.Y.

A.B.C.D.E.F.G.H.I.K. L.M.N.O.P.Q.R.S.T. U.W.X.

In the name of the Father, and of the Sonne, and of the holye Ghoste; So be it.

Children in the 17th century didn't have notebooks like the ones used in school today; they used hornbooks instead.

never required such punishment. In addition to Latin, Cotton Mather studied Hebrew and Greek. By the time he turned 12, he'd already read the New Testament in Greek.

Cotton Mather seemed to be well on his way to following in the footsteps of his famous family. But there was one problem—Cotton Mather stuttered and stammered. When he tried to speak, the words would not come out. Some have said it was because his brilliant mind was running so rapidly, his voice could not keep up.

This problem didn't seem to be a particularly devastating one to the boy. At 12 years old, he enrolled at Harvard College. One of the youngest students ever to attend the prestigious school, he settled upon a study of science and medicine. Cotton wanted to be a physician.

When Cotton Mather graduated from Harvard in 1678, he was only 15. At the commencement ceremonies, the president of Harvard, Urian Oakes, singled out Cotton Mather for special praise:

Mather is named Cotton Mather. What a name! I beg pardon, Gentlemen, I should have said what Names! . . . If he brings back and represents the Piety, the Erudition, the elegant Ability, the Sound Sense, the Prudence, and the Dignity of his Grandfathers . . . he may be said to have gained success; nor do I lack hope but that in this youth Cotton and Mather in fact as well as in name will unite and live again.

The legacy of Cotton Mather's family would follow the young man everywhere he went.

Cotton's father was the preacher of Boston's Second Church, also called North Church. Two years after graduating from Harvard, Cotton preached a sermon there himself. Later he served as pastor when his father was away.

2

Man of Religion

Following graduation, Cotton Mather turned to teaching. He taught his younger siblings, as well as a few other pupils. Often he prayed about his speech impediment. It was during this time that one of his old schoolmasters, Elijah Corlet, came to visit. Perhaps this elderly man understood Cotton's desire to preach. At any rate, he instructed Cotton Mather to compare his speaking with singing, "for as in singing there is no one who stammers, so by prolonging your pronunciation you will get an habit of speaking without hesitation."

Cotton Mather practiced a more deliberate speech pattern and soon the stammering was gone.

Now there was nothing to keep him out of the pulpit. Two years after his graduation he preached his first sermon in what had once been his grandfather's church in Dorchester. The next week he preached in his father's church, Second Church (also known as North Church) in Boston. He also preached at First Church, in the pulpit of Richard Mather, his paternal grandfather, who had died some 11 years earlier.

The first position offered to Cotton Mather was from a church in New Haven, Connecticut. However, Cotton had accepted a position as an assistant at his father's church. He became a close working partner and **confidant** of his father for many years to come.

Cotton Mather's association with Harvard continued when he received his master's degree there at age 19. A few years later his father became president of Harvard. Increase Mather fulfilled this position without leaving his pulpit at North Church, but by making periodic visits to Cambridge.

One of the youngest students ever enrolled at Harvard, Cotton graduated at the age of 15 and earned his master's degree at 19. While lots of new buildings now surround the campus, many of the original structures are still standing.

Due to Cotton Mather's many extensive writings, including his diaries and journals, much is known about his life, his actions, and his thoughts. For Cotton Mather and most Puritans of that time, church and religion was not an extra activity in their lives. It was, in fact, the very core of their being. They lived out their relationship with God in everything they said and did. Despite being described by some as stiff and straight-laced, the Puritans were emotional about their love of God and their desire to serve Him. Cotton Mather was a good example of this devotion. He often recorded his sins and his longing for forgiveness, as well as his love for God and Jesus.

As senior pastor, Increase Mather made very few calls on his parishioners. He felt his time was better spent in prayer, writing, and study. His son, however, felt differently. From the very start, the tender-hearted Cotton Mather chose to take his ministry outside the church and into the homes of the people. He visited the poor and the sick. He was not afraid to associate with those whom he considered "sinners." Whether it was a debtor, thief, pirate, murderer, or a condemned man on his way to the gallows,

Cotton Mather prayed with them all.

Across Boston Bay, in Charleston, lived a prosperous merchant by the name of Phillips. Phillips was an upstanding member of the church and served as a colonel in the local militia. The Mathers were aware that this good man had a marriageable daughter named Abigail. Cotton Mather's journal shows that he fell deeply in love with Abigail Phillips and prayed often for guidance during their courtship. The two were married on May 4, 1686. Cotton Mather was 23 years old; Abigail was 16.

After living a short time in the Phillips's home, the couple eventually moved into the house where Cotton was born, which had belonged to John Cotton. It was located close to the church and Cotton's neighbors were his father and mother and siblings.

In colonial times, many babies did not survive the first year. This was due mostly to disease and lack of medical knowledge. And so it was with Cotton and Abigail's first child, a daughter whom they had named after her mother. Upon baby Abigail's death, Cotton Mather was deeply grieved.

During this particular time, things were not going well between the New England colony and the motherland, England. For more than 55 years, Massachusetts Bay had been governed by a charter granted by the English crown. This charter allowed the citizens to govern themselves. In 1660 the new regime in England demanded that the charter be returned. The colonists ignored the demand. Finally, England's Catholic king, James II, had the charter revoked. That means the laws were no long in force.

The king appointed a royal governor, Sir Edmund Andros, to rule over all of New Eng-

In colonial times following the birth of a baby, visitors came to what was called a "sitting-up" visit. Cakes and wine were served and visitors wore their best attire. Gifts and trinkets were given to the nurse; and perhaps a pincushion was presented to the mother. Babies were given strange-sounding names such as Waitstill, Experience, Desire, and Unite.

land. With him came priests of the Church of England. This was the type of tyranny that the Puritans had come to America to escape. Governor Andros declared that all the land the colonists owned belonged to the British Crown. Both Cotton Mather and his father spoke boldly against the governor, which caused them to come into great disfavor.

In desperation, the colonists called upon Increase Mather to sail to England to try to straighten things out. Before Increase could leave the governor attempted to arrest him, but Increase escaped unharmed.

While his father was away, the responsibility of pastoring the large North Church fell on Cotton Mather's young shoulders. In spite of his youth, Cotton had become a confident preacher with full command of the pulpit. His listeners, sometimes numbering as high as 1,500 people at a time, hung on his every word.

Many months were required for the diplomatic work to be accomplished in England.

Even though Increase Mather was a great states-man, there were many obstacles to overcome. James II had been removed from power and William III and Mary II took the throne in 1688. This meant that Increase was forced to negotiate with new rulers.

During times when he was not involved in courtly duties, Increase purchased books on science and became acquainted with those who were members of the Royal Society of London for Improving Natural Knowledge. Since he was still president of Harvard, he sought out wealthy Englishmen to obtain funds for the school.

When Increase returned to New England many colonists were disappointed that instead of having the original charter restored, a new one had been created. The new charter fell short of the old since it required that there be a governor of New England by royal appointment. Now the people could no longer elect their own governor. The new governor was Sir William Phips. Of him, Cotton wrote in his journal, "The Governour of the Province is not my Enemy, but one whom I baptised, Namely Sir William Phips . . . one of my dearest Friends."

Even though both Mathers approved of Sir William, he would later prove to be a problem for them as well as the colonies.

A combination of political and religious factors caused seemingly minor incidents to flare into a series of witch trials and persecutions. This painting depicts the trial of George Jacobs, one of the people who was found guilty and hanged.

The Salem Witch Trials

3

In spite of his English title, Sir William Phips was a New Englander from Maine. The title of Sir was given when he recovered wealth from a sunken Spanish ship and returned the gold and jewels to England. In 1690 Phips was brought into full membership in the Puritan Church. The sea captain made a long confession of faith that was read aloud to the congregation of North Church. Cotton Mather was the one who baptized the first royal governor and admitted him to Communion.

One of the first duties that fell upon Phips when he returned from England with Increase was to tend to the problems that had arisen in Salem Village—

problems that involved witchcraft and evil spirits. Located about 14 miles from Boston, Salem Village was a small town outside of Salem proper (now called Danvers).

During the 1600s nearly everyone believed in witches and witchcraft, and had done so for centuries. In England, Sweden, and Europe, thousands of condemned witches had been put to death. Some were cruelly tortured to make them confess their "crimes."

The evidence of the work of witches was thought to be everywhere. If a person had an epileptic child, it seemed certain this strange illness was caused by witches. If a house caught fire, or if a cow acted oddly, witches were blamed. Any unusual phenomenon was attributed to the work of witches. In the 1600s this was not considered superstitious; it was believed to be fact.

The Puritans believed that before they came to America, Satan had ruled the area. For this reason they thought Indians were "bedeviled." Also during this time, slaves shipped from the

West Indies brought with them ideas about magic, superstitions, and voodoo.

A new wave of books imported from England revived an interest in black magic, fortune-telling, palmistry, and other mysterious workings. Cotton Mather was disturbed by this development. He wrote, "It is to be confessed and bewailed, that many Inhabitants of New-England, and Young People especially, had been led away with little Sorceries, wherein they did secretly those things that were not right against the Lord their God." He felt the devils had been "played with," and thus they broke out.

The witch scare in Salem Village began with a few girls seeming to show symptoms of being bewitched and blaming it on people whom they disliked. From this small beginning flared a wildfire of hysteria, as each person tried to outdo the others in being bewitched.

In the summer of 1692 Governor Phips appointed a special court in Salem with presiding judges of high regard. The accused people, however, were allowed no counsel and the judges were not bound to accept the verdicts of the jury. Charges were brought against more than 200 people. Many of them were jailed, and 55 of those admitted their guilt. This was no doubt an attempt at being set free. By September the trials were over and 19 people had been hanged.

While it was said in later years that Cotton and Increase Mather were to blame for some of the hysteria, that may not be totally true. First of all, both Increase and Cotton were interested in science. They studied natural phenomena and realized that strange occurrences stemmed from causes other than witchcraft. Eight years before the Salem witch trials, Increase wrote, "Many innocent persons have been put to death under the notions of witchcraft, whereby much innocent blood hath been shed." And in his book *Cases of Conscience Concerning Evil Spirits,* Increase wrote, "It were better that ten suspected witches should escape, than one innocent Person should be condemned."

Rebecca Nurse, a respected member of the community, was at first found innocent of witchcraft but the verdict was changed to guilty. Nurse declared, "I can say before my eternal Father that I am innocent." Despite her declaration she was excommunicated and hanged.

Cotton agreed fully. On several occasions he warned against accepting what is called "spectral evidence," which means taking one person's

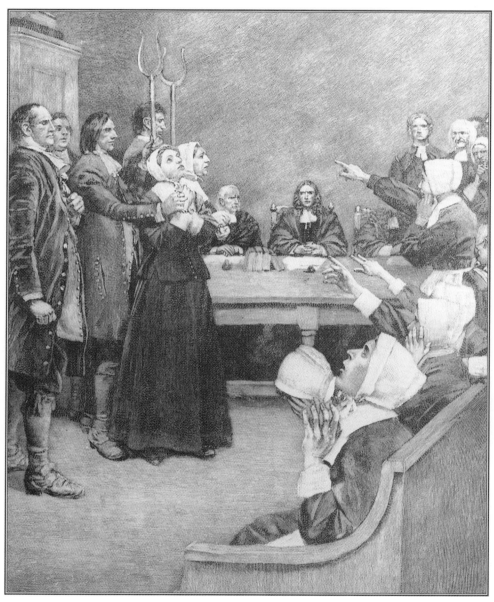

As the hysteria increased, more and more people appeared to show symptoms of "bedevilment," often claiming that particular people had used witchcraft to make them ill.

testimony as fact. He believed that spectral evidence should by no means be admitted. Cotton wrote letters to the judges, encouraging them not to use the death penalty. His idea was to scatter the accused witches rather than allowing them to remain in one group. He went so far as to offer to take six into his home.

At other times, he and his wife had taken "bewitched" persons into their home for treatment, such as the children of John Goodwin. Weeks of devoted care by the Mathers and kindly neighbors included a healthy diet, rest, quiet, and continual prayer. All four daughters were restored to "normal." However, his suggestions regarding the accused witches of Salem were ignored.

The Salem witch trials came to a sudden halt when Governor Phips returned from fighting the Indians in Maine to find that his own wife was accused of being a witch. After conferring with both Increase and Cotton Mather, Phips ordered an end to the special court and ordered

A memorial to the victims of the Salem witch trials reminds visitors today to practice tolerance and understanding. The names of all the people who were hanged spiral outward from the center.

the remaining condemned persons be released. Graves had actually been dug for five of those who were convicted. All were **reprieved**.

In September 1692 Cotton Mather met with John Higginson, William Stoughton, Stephen Sewall, and Samuel Sewall in Boston to discuss publishing a report of the Salem witch trials. This report, entitled *The Wonders of the Invisible World,* praised the Salem judges but condemned convictions based on spectral evidence. Unfortunately, in later years, this book served to tie Cotton Mather's name to the trials in a negative way. In another equally unfortunate event, Cotton Mather attended the execution of the Reverend George Burroughs, which again connected his name to the trials.

In spite of these two incidents, Cotton Mather did not fan the flames of hysteria in the Salem witch trials. Instead, he and his father were among those who helped bring it to an end.

Views of the North End of Boston in New England America and of Charles Town taken from the Hill ... of the Bea...

Boston continued to grow as more people settled there and more businesses developed. From a coastal village of a few thousand people, Boston became a bustling city filled with many different shops and industries.

4

Authorship and Family Tragedy

The busy port city of Boston was rapidly changing in the last part of the century. As the population grew, fewer people were now Puritans. Less looked solely to the Puritan preachers for guidance.

Cotton Mather saw that the power of the church was eroding, and he fought hard to prevent it from happening. Governor Phips was not always much help in this area. Phips was headstrong and wanted to do things his way. His mismanagement of the affairs of the colony became so serious that he was recalled to England in 1694 to answer the charges against him. While he was there awaiting his trial, Phips died.

From there, matters went from bad to worse. Cotton Mather began to work for Joseph Dudley to become governor. Cotton had once been strongly against Dudley during the time that Governor Andros was in office, but times had changed. Dudley's son, Thomas, was now a Harvard graduate. Cotton Mather may have thought that Joseph Dudley's loyalties had returned to the church. He was wrong. Within a few years of becoming governor, Joseph Dudley was one of the most hated men in the colony. Neither Cotton Mather nor his father approved of Dudley's actions or his decisions. It was becoming apparent that the Puritan leaders had less power and less say in political affairs.

In spite of these negative developments, the industrious Cotton continued to work extremely hard. He was a voracious reader, continually added to his already growing library. His study was one of his favorite places. There his reading, writing, and praying could proceed for long hours—sometimes into the late night and early mornings. He was known for keeping long prayer vigils and times of fasting. His detailed diaries record many of these prayer times, as well as what he thought were specific answers to his prayers.

Many of his books and papers were published during this time. Cotton Mather could write in seven languages, and had also mastered the Iroquois Indian language. He wrote a religious tract for sailors and an Indian primer. Since he felt a growing concern regarding impostors coming into the city pretending to be preachers, he wrote against this problem as well.

In 1700 Increase and Cotton Mather were faced with a disturbing situation regarding the church. Several men from the faculty of Harvard were making radical changes to the established ways of the Congregational Church. Their plan was to do away with the public testimony as a **prerequisite** for admission to church membership. Instead, they felt that each person should have a saving religious experience. This was a drastic change.

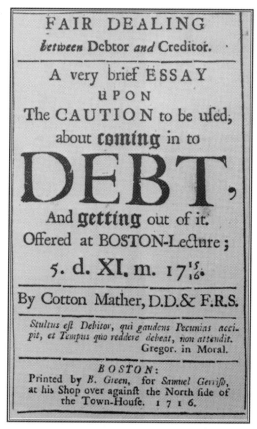

FAIR DEALING
between Debtor *and* Creditor.

A very brief ESSAY
υ P O N
The CAUTION to be uſed,
about **coming** in to

DEBT,

And **getting** out of it.
Offered at BOSTON-Lecture;

5. d. XI, m. 17¹⁵⁄₁₆.

By Cotton Mather, D.D.& F.R.S.

*Stultus eſt Debitor, qui gaudens Pecunias acci-
pit, et Tempus quo reddere debeat, non attendit.*
Gregor. in Moral.

BOSTON:
Printed by B. Green, for Samuel Gerriſh,
at his Shop over againſt the North ſide of
the Town-Houſe. 1 7 1 6.

Cotton Mather published a number of works, the most important of which recounts the history of the Plymouth settlement. This is a title page of a work of his from 1716.

These men founded a fourth and more **liberal** Congregational Church in Boston. The Brattle Street Church, as it was called, appointed Benjamin Colman as their pastor. Like Cotton Mather, Colman had studied under Ezekiel Cheever and was a Harvard graduate. During time spent in London, Colman was ordained a Presbyterian minister. In Mather's eyes, Colman was not a Puritan.

Cotton Mather wrote a firm protest against these actions. However, proving that he was not inflexible, Mather stopped the presses after the first sheet was printed. Instead, he approached the Brattle Street Church regarding a **compromise**.

Fortunately, Colman and his church leaders accepted the compromise agreement and differences were forgotten. In fact, the two churches kept public fasts together and eventually both Cotton Mather and his father preached in the pulpit of the Brattle Street Church. Through the years, Cotton Mather and Benjamin Colman became close friends.

The times were not without problems in Cotton Mather's home. In the summer of 1702 his dear wife, Abigail, became ill with tuberculosis. Nurses were with her around the clock. For many weeks she suffered, improving for a time and then relapsing.

At this same time, eight-year-old Nibby, five-year-old Nancy, and three-year-old Increase (named for his grandfather) came down with the dreaded smallpox. The house was so full of illness, even Cotton's study was turned into a sickroom. Eventually all three of the children recovered, but on December 1, 1702, Abigail died.

In his journal he wrote, "I had never yet seen such a black Day in all the Time of my pilgrimage. *The Desire of my Eyes* is this day to be taken from me." In a love poem dedicated to his wife, he wrote these sentimental lines: "Go then, my Dove, but now no longer mine; Leave Earth and now in heavenly Glory shine." The two had been married for 16 years.

Abigail never lived to see one of her husband's most important books be published. This huge leather-bound, 800-page book was titled *Magnalia Christi Americana* (The Mighty Deeds of Christ in America). The book was published in London. As important as this book was, it was not reprinted in America until some 118 years later. Then it was produced in two more manageable volumes.

This book gives all the historical facts, as Cotton Mather knew them, from the Pilgrim settlement at Plymouth to the year in which the book was published. He told what happened, why events occurred, and what the situations were like during certain times. He described the men of church and state. The massive book took four years to write.

This book was one of the most valuable of its time and one that historians have often referred to since. Much of what is known of the Plymouth settlement and its famed leaders comes from *Magnalia*. Also included are biographies of John Eliot, who preached tirelessly among the American Indians, and Sir William Phips, the late royal governor of the colony.

The one thing that Cotton Mather had hoped this book might help him gain was still held from him—the position of president of Harvard College. It is clear from his diaries that he very much wanted this position, which his father had held before him. However, this was a time when the Mathers were falling from favor in the elite circles of Harvard. While Cotton Mather was forward-looking in fields such as science, he was hopelessly tied to the past in church matters. He insisted that Harvard retain

Cotton hoped to become president of Harvard, a position his father had held. Modern-day Harvard is much larger and even more prestigious, but it was already quite important in Mather's time.

the Puritan traditional beliefs, but the college's leaders did not agree.

Another hindrance to Cotton Mather's appointment as president of Harvard was Governor Joseph Dudley. Differences between the governor and the Mathers had grown considerably. When Dudley appointed John Leverett as president of Harvard in 1707, Cotton was extremely disappointed. In a bitter letter, he reminded Dudley that it had been Mather's influence that gained him his position in the first place. Mather went on to accuse Dudley of bribery and corruption. He named several irregularities in both the civil and military affairs of Massachusetts Bay. On the same day, Increase Mather sent a similar letter, likewise naming specific accusations against the governor. It was clear at this point that the Mathers' power was decreasing in the political arena.

Despite his strong religious leanings, Cotton Mather was also interested in the study of science and medicine, and did not feel that science and religion were in conflict.

Man of
Science

Now a widower with four young children, Cotton Mather wanted a wife. He didn't have to look far. A 30-year-old widow by the name of Elizabeth Hubbard lived only two houses away. Cotton Mather described her as "a Gentlewoman of Piety and Probity and a most unspotted Reputation; a Gentlewoman of good Witt and Sense, and Discretion at ordering a Household; a Gentlewoman of incomparable Sweetness in her Temper, and Humor; a Gentlewoman honourably descended and related; and a very **comely** person."

The two were married in the summer of 1703. They would have six children together, only one of whom was still living when Cotton Mather died.

While Cotton Mather's level of influence was decreasing at home, a recognition of his fame came from abroad. In 1710 Glasgow University in Scotland conferred upon him its degree of doctor of divinity. Letters from scholars arrived testifying to the esteem in which Cotton Mather was held as a writer and scholar.

In this same year another of his books was published. While it was smaller than *Magnalia,* it became one of his most popular works. The book had a very long title but became known simply as *Bonifacius,* which is Latin for "Doer of Good." Some referred to the book as "Essays to Do Good." Published in Boston, *Bonifacius* went through many reprints in America. The book made "humble proposals of unexceptional methods" to business persons, merchants, and civil servants. Separate chapters were addressed to ministers, schoolmasters, magistrates, and physicians, and there was even a chapter for rich men. For instance, the book encouraged

Cotton received a doctor of divinity degree from Scotland's Glasgow University in 1710. Although this particular structure dates from 1870, the university itself was established in 1450.

schoolmasters not to beat or spank the students.

Bonifacius demonstrated Cotton Mather's deep commitment to the community. Always concerned for the less privileged, he went so far as to suggest that wealthy men give funds so that poor children might have an education. The main theme of the book was human decency—people caring for other people.

Cotton Mather lived out what was written on the pages of this book. Often he found himself in financial straits simply because he gave so much to charity. He maintained a school for Indians, he gave money to an elderly schoolmaster who was poor and crippled, and as he suggested in his book, he gave money for a poor child's schooling.

Cotton Mather was especially soft-hearted when it came to children. Often he would ride to outlying towns to preach. When he did, he always chose a young preacher to accompany him. The two would share religious ideas and prayers as they traveled from village to village. When he came into the town to preach, he would ask for a "play-day" for the children, that they might be excused from school.

Bonifacius helped many people of that time.

One of the most powerful testimonies to the effect of the book came years later (in 1784) from the elderly Benjamin Franklin. In a letter to Cotton Mather's son, Samuel, Franklin wrote, "When I was a boy, I met with a book entitled, 'Essays to Do Good.' . . . Several leaves of it were torn out, but the remainder gave me such a turn of thinking, as to have an influence on my conduct throughout life . . . and if I have been, as you seem to think, a useful citizen, the public owed all to the advantages of that book."

In addition to being community-minded, Cotton Mather gave much thought to science as well. His studies in science and medicine at Harvard were not wasted. Contrary to many **theologians** of his time, Cotton did not feel that science and religion were in conflict.

While in England, Increase Mather had become friends with scientists and later formed a scientific society in Boston. Cotton was a member of this society. Many of the scientists in England were highly curious about the natural

One of Cotton Mather's most popular books, *Bonifacius,* was to have a very strong influence on another important colonial leader, Benjamin Franklin.

history of the New World and Cotton was pleased to supply as much information as he possibly could.

When Dr. John Woodword, a geologist of London, wrote and asked Cotton Mather to supply information about North American fossils, Mather did so willingly. Because of this and many other reports, Cotton Mather was recognized as a man of scientific **attainments**. In 1713 he was made a **fellow** of the esteemed Royal Society of London. He was the only American clergyman who had ever received this high honor. From 1712 through 1724 he kept a steady stream of scientific reports in the mails to London. He told of animals that were not found in England, such as the muskrat, moose, sea lion, wild turkey, and eagle. There were vivid descriptions of the huge flocks of pigeons, some of which covered almost a mile. A neighbor of Cotton's killed a dozen birds with one shot.

Weather was also an interest. Cotton Mather closely observed and recorded such things as an

Although Cotton never attended a meeting of the Royal Society, its members recognized his scientific achievements and he was made a fellow of the organization.

eclipse in the fall of 1717 and a great blizzard that same winter. Religious thinkers of the day spoke of the wind as being caused by the movement of angels' wings and tides being caused by an angel's foot in the middle of the ocean. Cotton Mather, however, realized these were natural phenomena. No doubt he'd often read his father's book, *Essay for the Recording of Illustrious Providences,* which discussed unusual storms at sea, magnetism, and earthquakes. Both Cotton and his father were far ahead of the times in their scientific thinking, which in turn provided enlightenment for others.

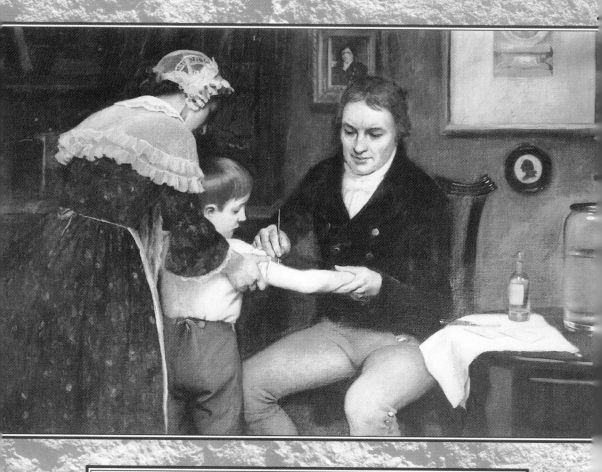

Cotton Mather was one of the first to recognize that inoculation could give immunity to a disease and save many lives. Many people, however, were frightened by this idea, and it took decades before most would put it into practice.

A Fruitful Life

Tragedy once again struck in the Mather household in 1713. On November 1 Elizabeth gave birth to a set of twins. They named the girl Martha and the boy Eleazer. A few days later Elizabeth and two-year-old daughter, Jerusha, came down with the measles. First Elizabeth died, then both the infant twins, and finally little Jerusha. Cotton Mather was grief-stricken once again. "My lovely Jerusha expires. She was Two years, and about Seven Months old. . . . Lord, I am oppressed; undertake for me." Cotton and Elizabeth had been married for 10 happy years.

As if this were not enough for one person to bear,

Cotton Mather's son Increase, named for his grandfather and nicknamed "Cresy," was proving to be a terrible problem. Both father and grandfather attempted to talk to and to pray for the younger Increase, but to no avail. "My miserable, miserable Son Increase!" Cotton wrote. "The wretch has brought himself under public Trouble and Infamy by bearing a part in a Night-Riot, with some detestable Rakes in the town."

Eventually, Mather attempted to disown this troublemaker son, but entries in his journals prove that he could never quite get the boy out of his heart and mind. Repeated entries show that he forgave Cresy many times. One consolation was found in his younger son Samuel, who, along with a few other boys, met in Cotton Mather's study for weekly prayer meetings and religious discussions.

Three years after Elizabeth's death, Cotton Mather once again took a wife. As it turned out, this union would be nowhere near as pleasant as the first two. Lydia Lee George, the widow of a merchant, became Cotton Mather's third wife in 1716. Cotton was 53. According to Mather, Lydia was not stable and suffered from times of deep depression alternating with fits of wild anger. This unpredictable behavior distressed the quiet, gentle Cotton Mather to no end.

Sickness and disease were constant companions to all those who lived during the colonial period. Disease knew no bounds; it visited saint and sinner, rich and poor, clergy and laypeople. Cotton Mather's household was no exception; he had survived smallpox as a child and saw two wives and several children succumb to various diseases. During his years at Harvard he had studied medicine and had never lost his interest in the subject. He was particularly fascinated with the scientific areas of medicine and was a believer in the **germ theory** of disease and its transmission. Through his correspondences with the Royal Society, he learned of a procedure known as **inoculation** to prevent smallpox. The procedure had been often used in Turkey and by

Cotton Mather urged everyone to be inoculated against smallpox but was highly criticized for this view. Finally, a doctor named Zabdiel Boylston joined efforts with Cotton to begin inoculating people.

natives in the West Indies. In fact Cotton's own slave, Onesimus, who had been a gift from his parishioners, showed him the scar on his arm from his inoculation.

In April 1721 a ship from Tortugas in the West Indies landed in Boston, bringing with it a new outbreak of smallpox. By May it had reached **epidemic** proportions, and fear drove hundreds from the city. Businesses closed down and the funeral bells tolled at all hours of night and day. In his diary Cotton Mather observed, "The grievous calamity of the smallpox has now entered the town."

Cotton Mather wrote a letter to the physicians of Boston urging inoculations for all those who were not yet stricken. He understood that smallpox was germ-carried, and the millions of germs were found in the pustules. The inoculation introduced live smallpox pus into a small incision. The result was a light sickness of about three days, after which the patient recovered and was forever immune.

The physicians turned on Mather in a vicious attack and the public accused him of perpetuating the disease. This "folk custom" as they called inoculation, had come from heathen lands and had been used by **atheists**. The thought made people frightened and angry.

One exception to the hysteria was young doctor named Zabdiel Boylston. He and Cotton Mather joined forces against the clamor of popular opinion. Boylston first inoculated his own son, Thomas, who recovered nicely. This was the very first inoculation ever to be administered in America. In July Dr. Boylston inoculated seven people, and in August, 17. While other doctors were only tending to the sick, Boylston was actually saving lives.

Zabdiel Boylston was born in Muddy River (now Brookline, Massachusetts). The son of a frontier doctor, he spent his childhood helping his father gather plants for ointments, tonics, and poultices. As an adult he owned and operated the largest **apothecary** shop in Boston. The shop was in Boston's Dock Square next to the Feather Store, just a short way from the famed Faneuil Hall.

Yet the opposition grew worse. Boylston was called before the magistrates three different times and told to stop his work, but he refused. Harshly written pamphlets publicly denounced Boylston and Mather. Cotton Mather wrote: "They rave, they rail, they blaspheme, they talk not only like Ideots, but also like Fanaticks, and not only the physician who began the Experiment, but I also am the object of their fury."

In the midst of all the turmoil, Samuel came to his father begging to be inoculated. What could his father do but agree? Samuel became so ill that he very nearly died. It is thought he may have already contracted the disease before the inoculation. Thankfully, he did recover.

In November, when the fury was at its height, a bomb was thrown into the window of Cotton Mather's house. Thankfully it hit the window casement, knocking off the lit fuse, or it might have leveled the entire house. In his journal he lamented the unfairness of the attacks. He claimed, that if people had listened to him, many lives would have been saved.

He was right. Of the 242 patients inoculated by Dr. Boylston, only six died. They were probably ones who had already been infected. By comparison, of the 5,889 in the city who contracted smallpox, 884 of them died. By February of 1722, the worst was over.

Dr. Zabdiel Boylston was eventually vindicated. He spent two years in London, where he lectured before the Royal College of Physicians. He also published a book about the inoculation experiment in America.

Two years after the smallpox epidemic, the aged Increase Mather fell ill. His illness was long and lingering but Cotton was a constant source of comfort. Increase Mather died August 23, 1723. The funeral was one befitting a man of Increase Mather's standing in the city of Boston. Leading ministers served as pall bearers. Other ministers and 160 Harvard students followed the casket through the winding Boston streets. After 84 years, the elder Mather was laid to rest.

At this time, Cotton Mather stepped into the position of senior pastor of North Church and a younger man, Reverend Joshua Gee, came on as the associate. Though nearing age 60, Cotton Mather continued his busy schedule of preaching, visiting the sick and needy, and extensively reading and writing . Eventually, Cotton Mather would author more than 400 works.

Throughout his lifetime, Cotton Mather kept up a great volume of correspondence with learned men in different countries. These men—ministers, mathematicians, philosophers, and scientists—were highly respected in their fields. In spite of the fact that Cotton Mather never left New England, he gained a global knowledge that was greater than most people in the Massachusetts colony.

In these later years, his son Increase continued to make Cotton Mather's life hard. His pain is evident from writings in his diary, "Oh! My Son Increase! My Son! My Son!" Finally in July 1724, it was reported that Cresy had been lost at sea. In September Cotton Mather preached a sermon on his son's death, which meant he had finally come to terms with this deep loss.

Meanwhile, other changes were taking place in the Christian community. In Northhampton, Massachusetts situated about 100 miles west of Boston, there were a series of revivals called "awakenings." These revivals were under the leadership of Jonathan Edwards. Many of the meetings took place outdoors, where hundreds of people would gather to hear the preaching. This type of church meeting was highly **unorthodox** and was frowned upon by many of the Puritan leaders. Although Cotton Mather saw only the begin-

During the time known as the Great Awakening, itinerant preachers traveled through the countryside holding meetings in barns, private homes, schools, and open pastures. They did this without permission from local pastors. The churches accused these evangelical pastors of causing disorderly commotions. But those whose lives were changed by the preaching called them "sweet visitations of the Lord."

nings of this movement, he was surprisingly liberal. He rejoiced that a new spirit of religion had come to the colonies.

In December 1727 Cotton Mather became ill. It looked as though he would not live to a ripe old age as his father had. For one as passionately religious as Cotton Mather had been all his life, death was not something to be feared. It was rather something to be welcomed. When son Samuel asked his father for a last word, Cotton Mather said, "Remember only that one word, *Fructuosus*" ("fruitful" in Latin). He died the day after his 65th birthday, on February 13, 1728.

Cotton's last words aptly described his life. He never stopped working for his community, his church, and his family. Hundreds of people attended his funeral, and many who had criticized him before his death now praised him. He had made his mark in religion, science, medicine, history, literature, and social reform. In that day and time no other person had as many or as varied accomplishments. To the best of his ability, Cotton Mather did what he knew to be right all the days of his life. He did indeed live up to the heritage of the names of Cotton and Mather.

GLOSSARY

apothecary a person who is trained in the preparation of drugs and medicines

atheist one who denies the existence of God

attainments something that is achieved, such as a skill or ability

comely having a pleasing appearance

compromise a settlement of differences where each side gives up some of its claims and agrees to some of the demands of the other

confidant a person to whom one confides personal matters or secrets

epidemic a contagious disease that spreads very rapidly

fathom a measure of water depth, about six feet

fellow a member of a learned society

germ theory the idea that diseases may be spread by minute organisms invisible to the naked eye

inoculation process to make a person immune to a disease by introducing bacteria or viruses into the body

liberal respectful of different people and ideas; tolerant

nonconformist someone who does not follow accepted customs, beliefs, or practices

prerequisite required as a prior condition

Puritans a group of English Protestants in the 16th and 17th centuries who wished to simplify ceremonies and creeds of the Church of England

reprieve to postpone or cancel punishment

theologian one who studies the nature of God and a person's relationship to God

unorthodox breaking away from tradition

vestments a garment such as a robe, indicating an office or standing

waning to decrease as in size, strength, or importance

CHRONOLOGY

1663 Cotton Mather is born in Boston, Massachusetts.

1664 Cotton's father, Increase, is ordained as
teacher of the Second (North) Church in
Boston.

1675–78 Cotton Mather attends Harvard at age 12,
one of the youngest students ever admitted.

1680 Mather enters the ministry; preaches his first
sermon, in the church of his grandfather
Richard Mather.

1685 Cotton becomes an associate with his father
at Second Church.

1686 Abigail Phillips and Cotton Mather are
married.

1692 Outbreak of the witch trials in Salem Village;
Mather objects vocally to the use of spectral
evidence and the use of the death penalty.

1702 After a lingering illness, Abigail dies of
tuberculosis. Mather's most important book,
Magnalia Christi Americana, is published; it
outlines in detail the history of the colonies
from Plymouth Rock to the present time in
Mather's life.

1703 Mather marries Elizabeth Hubbard.

1713 Mather is elected as a Fellow of the Royal Society of London.

1721 Smallpox epidemic ravages Boston; first inoculation is given by Dr. Zabdiel Boylston to his son, Thomas; Mather is slandered due to his approval of the inoculation.

1724 Mather's son, Increase (Cresy), is lost at sea.

1726 Elizabeth, Mather's 22-year-old daughter, dies; she is his 13th child to die.

1727 Revivals called "awakenings," touched off by Jonathan Edwards, sweep through New England; the evangelistic revivals split the existing church.

1728 Cotton Mather dies with his son Samuel at his side; he is buried at the old Copp's Hill Burying Ground.

COLONIAL TIME LINE

1607 Jamestown, Virginia, is settled by the English.

1620 Pilgrims on the *Mayflower* land at Plymouth, Massachusetts.

1623 The Dutch settle New Netherlands, the colony that later becomes New York.

1630 Massachusetts Bay Colony is started.

1634 Maryland is settled as a Roman Catholic colony. Later Maryland becomes a safe place for people with different religious beliefs.

1636 Roger Williams is thrown out of the Massachusetts Bay Colony. He settles Rhode Island, the first colony to give people freedom of religion.

1682 William Penn forms the colony of Pennsylvania.

1688 Pennsylvania Quakers make the first formal protest against slavery.

1692 Trials for witchcraft are held in Salem, Massachusetts.

1712 Slaves revolt in New York. Twenty-one blacks are killed as punishment.

1720 Major smallpox outbreak occurs in Boston. Cotton Mather and some doctors try a new treatment. Many people think the new treatment shouldn't be used.

1754 French and Indian War begins. It ends nine years later.

1761 Benjamin Banneker builds a wooden clock that keeps precise time.

1765 Britain passes the Stamp Act. Violent protests break out in the colonies. The Stamp Act is ended the next year.

1775 The battles of Lexington and Concord begin the American Revolution.

1776 Declaration of Independence is signed.

FURTHER READING

Chadwick, Bruce. *Infamous Trials*. Philadelphia: Chelsea House, 1997.

Fradin, Dennis. *The Massachusetts Colony*. Chicago: Children's Press, 1987.

Lutz, Norma Jean. *Smallpox Strikes!* Uhrichsville, Ohio: Barbour & Co, 1997.

Maestro, Betsy. *The New Americans: Colonial Times 1620–1689*. New York: Lothrop, Lee & Shepard Books, 1998.

Terkel, Susan Neiburg. *Colonial American Medicine*. New York: Franklin Watts, 1993.

Wroble, Lisa A. *Kids in Colonial Times*. New York: PowerKids Press, 1997.

INDEX

77

INDEX

PICTURE CREDITS

ABOUT THE AUTHORS

NORMA JEAN LUTZ, who lives in Tulsa, Oklahoma, has been writing professionally since 1977. She is the author of more than 250 short stories and articles as well as over 30 books–fiction and nonfiction. Of all the writing she does, she most enjoys writing children's books.

Senior Consulting Editor **ARTHUR M. SCHLESINGER, JR.** is the leading American historian of our time. He won the Pulitzer Prize for his book *The Age of Jackson* (1945) and again for *A Thousand Days* (1965). This chronicle of the Kennedy Administration also won a National Book Award. He has written many other books including a multi-volume series, *The Age of Roosevelt*. Professor Schlesinger is the Albert Schweitzer Professor of the Humanities at the City University of New York, and has been involved in several other Chelsea House projects, including the REVOLUTIONARY WAR LEADERS biographies on the most prominent figures of early American history.